MAGIC TRICKS

SECRETS OF THE MASTER MAGICIAN

IAN ADAIR

ISBN: 0–7858–0497–8

This book was designed and produced by
Quintet Publishing Limited

Creative Director: Terry Jeavons
Designer: Chris Dymond
Project Editor: Judith Simons
Editor: Louise Bostock
Photographer: Tim Cox
Illustrator: Rob Shone
Jacket Design: Nik Morley

Typeset in Great Britain by
Central Southern Typesetters, Eastbourne

Produced in Australia by Griffin Colour

Published by Chartwell Books
A Division of Book Sales, Inc.
P.O. Box 7100
Edison, New Jersey 08818–7100

Contents

INTRODUCTION – WELCOME TO MAGIC

Welcome to the wonderful world of magic! Welcome to meeting magicians and sharing their magical secrets. And welcome to the pages of this book, which I hope will put you on the road to success, whether magic or conjuring be an enjoyable hobby or your destined profession.

Magic or conjuring offers bewilderment, colour, excitement and mystery. But it must always *entertain* those who are involved, either as spectators or participants. Perfecting magical techniques and putting them into practice is one thing, but it is quite another to actually go out and face an audience, knowing that they are waiting to be entertained. Pure bewilderment is not enough, and the student of magic will soon realize that clever patter, rehearsed movements and keeping control of numbers are as important as the secrets of the tricks he or she has to execute.

This book shows that in magic, there are many fascinating avenues to explore. There are magic dealers who specialize in selling professional properties; there are magic conventions, dinners and events, social functions attended by all the stars of magic. Magic conventions offer seminars, lectures and demonstrations and teach-ins, many of which are invaluable to the novice. There are magic clubs and societies, large and small, all over the world. The reader of this book will also soon realize that there are many branches of magic, and that each branch suits particular personalities. This book covers several of the major branches of magic, giving details of important techniques and a host of individual tricks to perfect. It also gives advice on presentation before an audience, large or small.

Buying a book of magic does not automatically make you a magician, but with practice and interest, you could go a long way.

★ THE RULES OF MAGIC ★

Every game, profession or organization has certain rules to adhere to; some we accept, some we like and others we dislike intensely.

The first, and perhaps only, rule of magic, is that a magician never gives away the secrets of magic. Magicians performing tricks never reveal the secrets after their performance. The audience's enjoyment of magic is to a certain extent due to the mystery of how the magic happened. To tell the secret of a trick is to deny the audience this enjoyment. The audience feel that although they were at first entertained, they have now been cheated, and quite rightly so. The first rule of magic is to keep the secret.

Can you keep a secret?

★ PRACTICE ★

Practice is the learning of individual effects and routines, and the rehearsal of a complete act from start to finish. Theatrical people use the word rehearsal as a run-through with a cast or partner, and a dress rehearsal is just as it should be on the night.

Professionals and amateurs alike joke that it will be all right on the night – but will it? The wise and discerning performer understands that only practice and attention to detail make for trouble-free performances. To achieve this, one must have patience, time and understanding.

I remember seeing a very enthusiastic student of magic rush into a performance without planning his programme. He fumbled, dropped items, forgot his patter lines and generally made a fool of himself. His appearance was good, his tricks and execution fair, but his presentation left much to be desired. He had forgotten to practice his movements, as well as his tricks. While it is admirable to perform a trick cleverly, it is unwise to disregard the way in which move-ments should be executed. There is nothing worse than seeing a clumsy magician, in the middle of his act, bending down to retrieve his apparatus, and setting it out again in front of his audience.

Practising in front of a mirror is good training, but not always the best. When working to a mirror, there is a tendency to stand in the same position, which means that a public performance could well appear static. I know of one young man who used his bedroom in which to practise his act. In front of the mirror, one by one, he discarded each trick – on the nearby bed. When he presented his act on stage before a live audience, there was no mirror, and there was certainly no bed. The performer had not worked out where he would discard all his unwanted apparatus. It was not all right on the night – his act was a flop.

Practise walking on and off, never turning your back to the audience, unless of course the effect or routine demands it. Taking a bow may seem easy, but can often look a farce when executed by someone who feels silly. When the trick has come to its climax, the performer needs to clearly signal this to the audience – a smile, arms opening upwards and a slight bow achieves the right effect for the wise performer who wants to go home that evening well and truly satisfied with his performance.

The wise student should practise each trick so much that he or she could almost perform them blindfolded. If the student aims to come over professionally, he or she must practise again and again, until every little detail is embedded in the mind. Slow, smooth and elegant hand gestures should also be practised. The magician should appear graceful and compelling, and should know how to handle spectators.

One top television magician told me that he has now practised his act so much that, while he appears in front of a live audience or before the cameras, he is thinking about what he is going to eat after the show! Now that's show business.

SELECTING THE
★ CORRECT BRANCH OF MAGIC ★

Some magicians present a mixed bag of tricks and illusions drawn from many different branches of magic, others specialize in one form – mentalism, say, or close-up magic. In making a choice of which field to enter, one must be careful. So often, enthusiastic beginners choose the wrong branches of magic to present, ending in disaster.

If you happen to like comedy magic – that is ordinary magic laced with comedy patter – then stick to it. Think again if you are someone who does not excite people very much and cannot tell funny jokes or stories. It could be that you will never be able to become a comedy magical entertainer.

If, on the other hand, you feel that your approach is better at reaching more mature audiences, a serving of mentalism may be the answer. If so, be sure you can deliver direct and dramatic lines. Make sure your face fits the picture. Do you look like a person who reads minds and predicts the future?

If you simply wish to be a jack of all trades, and want to entertain your friends, you cannot be categorized in any way – you are just a general magician. Relax, look at the tricks in this book, learn them and select the ones you like best. Practise each trick and master the various methods of presentation, then use the ones you are more confident at performing and go out to entertain your public. Select the times when you wish to perform and never perform under pressure.

MAGIC DEALERS –
THEIR ROLE IN SERVING
★ THE MAGICIAN ★

The magic dealer is a maker of magic; he makes magic in various materials, markets his products, and then sells his wares through various channels. Most dealers offer a mail-order service, which they advertise in magazines; some larger concerns issue their own catalogues or magazines in which they advertise their range of theatrical properties.

Having been associated with magic dealing for over three decades, I find that magic dealers can be listed in three categories. First is the magic shop, often a joke shop, selling whoopee cushions, novelties and toys. Only one small section of the shop may be de-voted to magic, or to the sale of professional conjuring props. The selection of items is usually very basic. Although some professional material is available, only classic effects are ordered by the proprietor who, incidentally, very rarely knows anything about the art of magic.

Second is the small mail-order firm, which usually advertises in magic magazines. Many do not have proper premises, and it is often hard to find those who do. Most magic dealers work from one room of their house, say a spare room which they have turned into a stockroom. Mail-order dealers send goods through the post, and some provide a fast and efficient service, even if they only advertise a small number of products within their range.

Third is the more professional magic dealer who works on a much larger scale. Such dealers have a good knowledge of what customers require and a wide range of products, classic and modern. Some publish their own magic magazine which furthers sales of their products. The professional magic dealer never relies upon the sales of jokes and novelties to enhance his sales of professional theatrical equipment.

JOINING MAGIC CLUBS
★ AND SOCIETIES ★

Magic is no different from any other hobby or profession in that there are many clubs, societies and organizations to join. The famous Magic Circle, formed in 1905, started with just a few magicians and, over a period of years, it has attracted more and more members so that there are now some 1,800 members across the world.

Membership of the Magic Circle depends on merit, and there is a strict hierarchy of membership. Associate members progress to full membership, eventually becoming associate and then full members of the Inner Magic Circle. The Magic Circle has its own meeting place in London, and magicians meet regularly to share ideas, discuss new tricks and hear visiting speakers.

A similar organization is the International Brotherhood of Magicians, with headquarters in the United States. Although larger than the Magic Circle, the International Brotherhood of Magicians has no regular meeting place. Members keep in touch with each other through the pages of the official magazine, *The Budget*, a monthly publication distributed only to members. The major event of the year is the Annual Convention, often attracting two thousand or more magicians. Lectures, dealers' demonstrations, gala shows, teach-ins, close-up sessions and many other interesting aspects of magic are planned each year to keep magicians informed and on their toes.

The majority of the smaller magic societies draw perhaps only 20 or 30 members from the local area, but they are all dedicated to learning and practising the art of magic.

Annual subscription fees differ from one club to the other; it is often the case that members of a small society are members of both the Magic Circle in London and the International Brotherhood of Magicians. Some magicians become members of several organizations connected with magic, so as to enjoy a well-balanced and varied outlook on what is happening in the world of magic.

Joining a magic club or society can be a most enjoyable experience, one shared by all members who participate, each endeavouring to elevate the craft to the highest standard possible.

SUBSCRIBING TO
★ MAGIC MAGAZINES ★

Most beginners do not realize that there are such things as magic magazines, produced especially for the student of magic, perhaps because they are not available from the newsagents. Such insiders periodicals are available on subscription only.

There are some 22 periodicals internationally available at the moment. Some appear quarterly and some monthly, but there is only one weekly magazine of magic – *Abracadabra*. Goodliffe the Magician, well known in his day, and still a name to conjure with, first published this magazine some 44 years ago. Today, Donald Bevan, who has been responsible for 30 years of continued production, has managed to release the magazine weekly without fail. Monthly magazines include *The Magigram*, a 72-page magazine of magic which is distributed worldwide; it covers 80 different countries, including the Soviet Union, and is printed on the premises of The Supreme Magic Company in the UK. The same company also produces a sister magazine *The Trixigram*, a publication which brings the magician news, views and reviews on the magic scene. A recent magazine of magic, *Alakazam*, is aimed at children's entertainers.

★ ADVERTISING AND PUBLICITY ★

The subject of promoting oneself as a performer arises once the student of magic has brought together a complete series of tricks, practised them until he or she is perfect, and has established a show ready for presentation to the public. There are many ways in which to promote and advertise. The most obvious place to start is the classified telephone directory or local newspaper. The advantages of these publications are relatively cheap advertising, in a restricted locale.

However you advertise, whether it be in magazines or newspapers, or even in the window of a local shop, your advertisement must be literate, informative, and well laid out. Poor copy material never results in bookings, and an over-elaborate ad confuses the public.

A very good method of obtaining superb publicity – for free– is to supply a story of news interest to the local or national press. Not only does a news story act as free advertising, it also takes up more space than the average ad, giving you even more exposure. Here is an example . . . One magician I know advertised every week, but without much success. One week he concocted a story that his magic rabbit had vanished from its hutch, and this received not only local but national coverage. He obtained more show bookings from that article alone than from all his paid advertisements.

Photographs, pictures, business cards, leaflets and flyers, and give-away trivia all help to promote you and your show. Balloons printed with your name, magic posters for the children to colour, magic 'money' to give away amuses and excites, and pictures of the rabbit which assisted you in the show simply makes them all want to take the printed card home.

Promoting your show can be as much fun as practising the tricks and presenting the act, yet in considering promotion one must always be aware that *you* are the commodity being promoted. In doing so, you must try to emphasize your better features and talents, but always tell the truth.

SIMPLE SLEIGHT OF HAND AND MANIPULATION

All accomplished magicians make sure that they have mastered sleight of hand. It is important for several reasons. First, your movements will appear more polished, even when using other props. Second, if such props let you down, you can always rely upon sleight of hand to get through. Third, your routines will be more varied and entertaining if sleight of hand sequences are introduced in between other effects.

A great deal of time and patience must be devoted to perfecting the techniques but, once mastered, your skills will be a source of great amusement to all. It is important to ensure that finger nails are cut and clean, and that sleeve cuffs are presentable.

★ CARDS ★

PALMING CARDS
· · · · ☆ ☆ ☆ · · · ·

Many of the card effects performed by magicians and manipulators are achieved by palming cards. Here are two classic card palms.

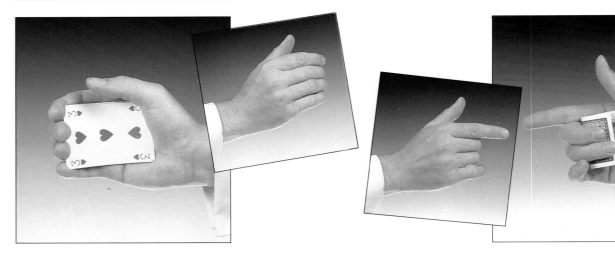

Flat-palm version

ABOVE Place the card flat in the palm of the hand and hold the card facing towards you. From the audience's viewpoint (see inset), the card cannot be seen and the hand position looks natural.

Curled-in version

ABOVE With the card held flat in the palm, curl the fingers in, bending the card over. Invisible to the audience, this version allows you to adopt a different hand position (see inset).

PRODUCING CARDS

· · · · ☆ ☆ ☆ · · · · ·

Producing single cards from the hand

First a card is seen between the fingers, next it is made to vanish and then reappear again.

1 Display the card to the audience.

2 Grip the sides of the card with the first and little fingers, bend the middle fingers down behind the card and use the thumb to pivot the card over . . .

3 . . . like this. Using the middle fingers to control the card, continue the move so that the card disappears from view to be held . . .

4 . . . in the back-palm position.

5 Hold the hand side-on to the audience and reverse the pivot.

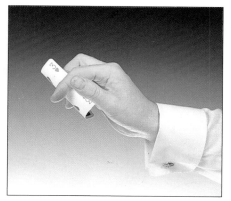

6 Use the fingers to draw the card into the palm position.

7 Hold the back of the hand towards the audience to show that the card has once again disappeared from view.

8 Repeat Steps 1 – 3 to bring the card to the back-palm position again.

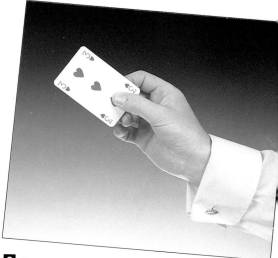

9 To produce the card, reach up into the air and at the same time pivot the card up into the hand.

Producing several cards from the hand

The same pivoting action is used to produce a succession of cards from a stack held secretly in the hand. Again, the effect is of cards being plucked from the air.

1 Hold the stack in the back-palm position and pivot the stack into the hand . . .

2 . . . like this.

3 Peel off the first card from the stack with the thumb and pivot the stack to the back-palm position . . .

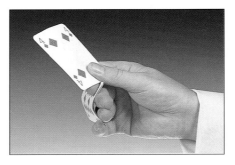

4 . . . like this.

5 Repeat the sequence, discarding the first card and producing a second and so on until the stack is exhausted.

Producing cards — a variation

Most magicians produce cards with the palm of the right or left hand facing the audience, plucking cards out of the air. In this variation the cards are produced while the left hand is clenched towards the audience.

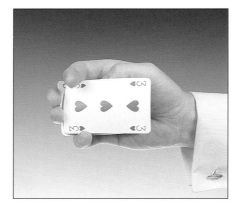

1 Conceal a stack of cards within the palm.

2 Grip the pack with the fingers. Peel off the first card with the thumb . . .

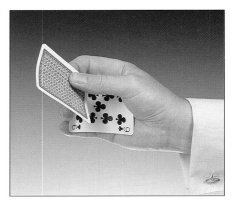

3 . . . and produce it to the audience between the thumb and first finger.

4 The audience's view of the produced card. Repeat the sequence to produce more cards, discarding each in turn.

★ VANISHING HALF A PACK ★

During card-manipulation routines, a neat vanish of half a pack is visually effective.

3 The back view showing the half pack held in the right hand behind the fan.

1 Display half a pack of cards, squared-up, in the left hand and fan the remainder of the pack in the right hand.

2 Obscure the left hand with the fan of cards, and secretly grip the half pack with the free fingers of the right hand. At the same time turn the left hand and form it into a fist.

4 From the front view again, open the left fist to show that the half pack has vanished and gather the entire pack together in the right hand.

Producing fans of cards

The back-palm position again plays a major part in producing fans of cards. The effect is that the magician produces a fan and drops it into a receptacle and then magically produces further fans from thin air, discarding each. In fact, each fan produced is split, with the majority of the cards being pivoted to the back-palm position ready to produce the next fans, while just a few of the top cards are discarded.

1 Fan the stack of cards towards the audience.

2 Curl the third and little fingers round the bottom of the fan to pivot the majority of the stack to the back-palm position . . .

3 . . . like this.

4 The start of the pivoting move seen from the back view.

5 The completion of the pivot, again from the back view, with the stack in back-palm position.

6 Discard the remaining few cards in the fan, then pivot the stack back into the hand to produce the next fan.

★ THIMBLES ★

PRODUCING THIMBLES
· · · · ☆ ☆ ☆ · · · ·

Producing a single thimble

A thimble is apparently plucked from the air to appear on the magician's thumb.

1 Secretly hold the thimble at the back of the hand in the finger-palm position, gripped between the first and third fingers, and present the hand palm-on to the audience.

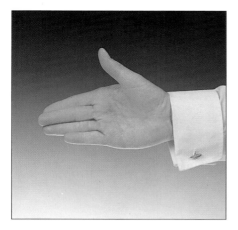

2 To the audience, the thimble is invisible.

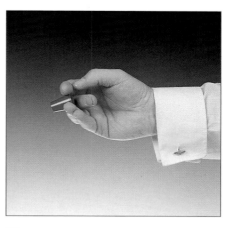

3 Pivot the thimble into the hand and . . .

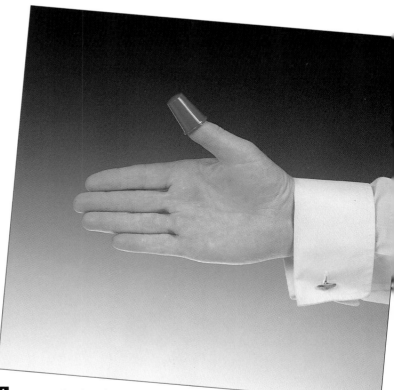

4 . . . onto the thumb as you apparently pluck the thimble from the air.

★ SHOWING THE HANDS EMPTY ★

This technique is also applied to the thumb-tip.

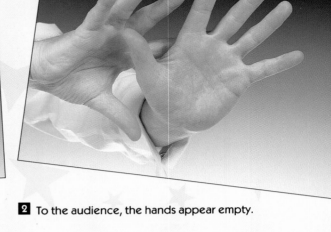

1 Conceal the first finger, wearing the thimble, behind the back of the opposite hand.

2 To the audience, the hands appear empty.

Producing a succession of thimbles

The thumb-crutch position, or thumb palm, is used to conceal a stack of thimbles.

ABOVE Grip a stack of thimbles in the fleshy part of the hand between thumb and first finger in the thumb-crutch position. To produce a succession of thimbles, one after the other, simply pivot a finger down onto the thimble on top of the stack, and repeat, passing the thimbles from one hand to another.

★ A THIMBLE HOLDER ★

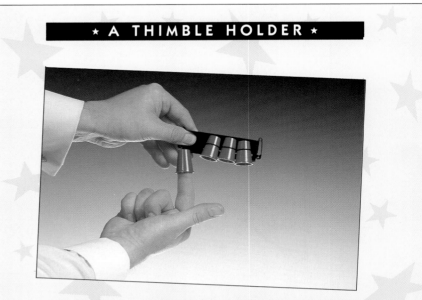

ABOVE The thimble holder is an aid which allows the performer to secretly and easily acquire one or more thimbles while leaving the hands free. The thimbles slide easily from the thimble holder; it is usually attached and concealed inside the jacket.

VANISHING THIMBLES
· · · · ☆ ☆ ☆ · · · ·

Poke-in thimble vanish

To make a thimble vanish in a convincing manner, this method is hard to beat.

1 Display the thimble on the first finger of the right hand and poke this finger into the left hand.

2 Seen from the rear view, as you close the left hand to form a fist, curl the thimble finger inwards, bringing the thimble into the thumb-crutch position.

3 To the audience, the left hand appears to be holding the first finger *and* the thimble.

4 Remove the first finger of the right hand and point towards the closed left fist to reinforce the suggestion that the thimble has been retained in the left hand.

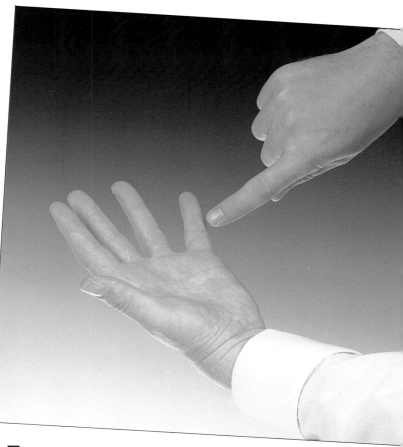

5 Open the left fist to complete the vanish. The thimble is still concealed in the right hand.

A simple thimble vanish

A thimble is thrown up into the air and magically vanishes.

1 Display the thimble on the first finger.

2 Make an upward throwing motion with the hand and at the same time curl the first finger towards the crutch of the thumb.

3 Seen from the rear view, immediately release the thimble and hold it in the thumb-crutch position.

4 To the audience, the hand, having completed the throw, appears empty.

★ BALLS ★

PALMING A BALL
· · · · ☆ ☆ ☆ · · · ·

Palm grip

A ball will adhere to the palm of the hand, if the hand is moist or has been smeared with a moisturizing cream.

ABOVE Seen from the rear, the ball clings to the palm. Keep the hand in a natural position, ensuring the ball is invisible to the audience.

Finger-grip palm

This variation allows the performer to adopt a different hand position.

ABOVE Seen from the rear, grip the ball between the palm and lower three fingers.

ABOVE To the audience, the hand position, with the index finger pointing, looks natural, and the ball is completely concealed.

VANISHING A BALL

· · · · ☆ ☆ ☆ · · ·

Here are three different vanishes to practise and master.

Take-away vanish

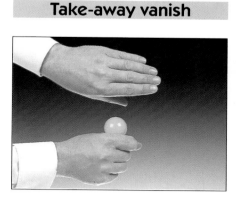

1 Rest the ball on top of the clenched right fist, and bring the left hand, held in a cupped fashion, towards the right as if to take the ball.

2 Pretend to take the ball away from the right fist and at the same time . . .

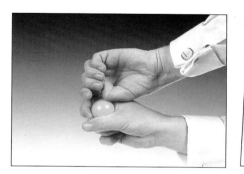

3 . . . drop the ball into the right fist (seen from the rear).

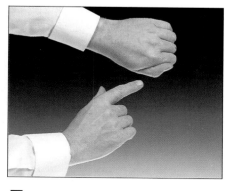

4 From the front again, with the ball in the finger-grip palm position, point to the left fist and . . .

5 . . . slowly open the fingers of the left hand to show the vanish.

6 The rear view shows the ball concealed in the right hand.

Poke-in vanish

1 Clench the left hand around ball, holding the fist side on to the audience so the ball is visible, and bring the right hand up underneath the left.

2 Poke the ball into the fist with the right thumb, allowing the right hand to cup underneath the left.

3 At the same time allow the ball to drop into the right hand (seen from the rear).

4 With the ball held in the finger-grip palm position, poke the 'ball' into the left fist again with the index finger, to reinforce the belief that the ball is still in the left hand.

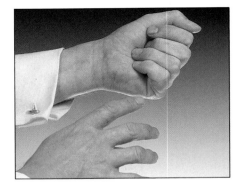

5 Turn the left hand over, and with the ball now held in the palm-grip position in the right hand . . .

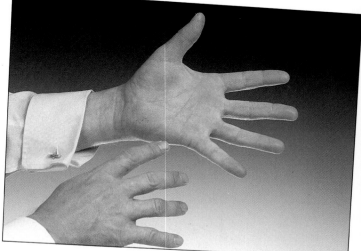

6 . . . slowly open the fingers of the left hand to reveal the vanish.

Lift-up vanish

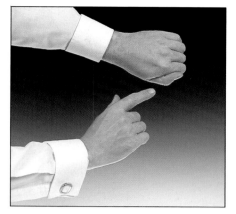

3 With the ball in the finger-grip palm position, point to the clenched left fist and . . .

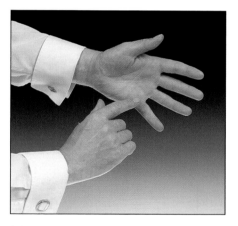

4 . . . slowly open the fingers of the left hand to reveal the vanish.

1 Hold the ball in the palm of the right hand and move the left hand towards it as if to take away the ball.

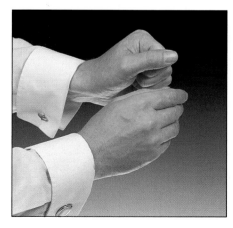

2 As the left hand supposedly grips away the ball, turn the right hand over so that the back of the hand points towards the audience, and retain the ball in this hand.

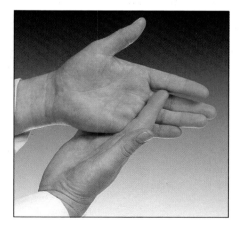

5 For a further effect, partially turn the right hand to face the audience, pivoting the ball behind the back of the open left hand.

★ COINS ★

PRODUCING AND VANISHING ★ A COIN ★

To produce a single coin out of the air, or indeed from someone's clothing, this method is simple and effective when put into action. Incidentally, the same coin can be vanished by reversing the procedure.

1 Secretly hold the coin at the back of the hand, gripped between the first and second fingers.

3 To produce the coin, pivot the fingers inwards and . . .

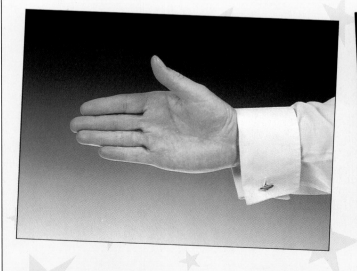

2 Show the hand palm-on so that the audience sees that it is apparently empty.

4 . . . use the thumb to bring the coin out from the back position so it appears for all to see.

★ PRODUCING SEVERAL COINS ★

1 Conceal a stack of coins within the crutch of the thumb.

2 Hold the hand palm-on so that the audience sees that the hand is apparently empty.

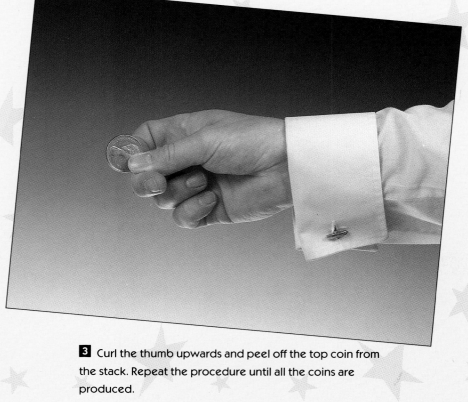

3 Curl the thumb upwards and peel off the top coin from the stack. Repeat the procedure until all the coins are produced.

CLEVER CARD TRICKS

It is not unusual for the beginner in magic to start with card tricks. I did when I was a boy magician and so did many of my magician friends. A pack of cards is inexpensive, and usually available at home anyway, which means that the budding magician is involved in little or no expense. Do not forget, however, that practice makes perfect.

Card tricks can be presented almost any-where – on a table, on the floor or even in the hands of the performer. Some magicians use a close-up mat to work on, the spread of cards showing up well against the flock-covered surface of a contrasting colour. Others prefer to use a bar counter or table.

As for the cards themselves, some magicians prefer cards which have a linen finish, others prefer the surfaces to be plastic-coated. Avoid using cheap, badly made cards. These tend to crack when even slightly bent and do not wear well. If using your own pack of cards, powder them on both sides with zinc stereate to make the complete pack easy to handle and perfect to fan. In selecting a pack for yourself, try and obtain one which has a common back design, of the type audiences are familiar with. Bent, torn and defaced cards never assist the performer, because audiences will automatically think these are blatant markings for the benefit of the performer.

UPON REFLECTION

· · · · ☆ ☆ ☆ · · · ·

This amazing card trick can be repeated several times without spectators detecting its secret.

Effect

A spectator is requested to select a card from a pack by pushing the blade of a table knife into it and noting the card above the blade. Needless to say, the performer correctly reveals the name of the chosen card.

Apparatus

A regular pack of cards and a table knife that has a shiny blade.

Working and Presentation

Ask a member of the audience to shuffle the pack of cards and then to hold the pack in his left hand, cards facing downwards. Hand the table knife to the spectator and ask him to select a card by pushing the blade in between any section of cards. Finally, ask the spectator to note the selected card above the knife blade.

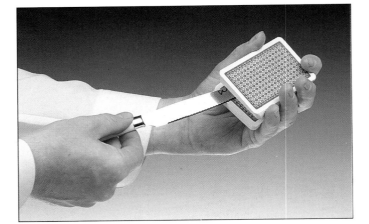

LEFT The selected card's suit and value is clearly reflected in the shiny knife blade.

Take the pack from the spectator and with the knife still lodged between the cards, lift the top portion so that you can secretly glimpse a reverse reflection of the suit and value of the selected card. The polished blade makes this possible and you need only lift the portion of cards slightly. However, it is important to position the knife blade towards the bottom left corner where the card's suit and value appears.

You can now reveal the name of the chosen card. Declare the colour of the suit first, then the value of the card, to make the presentation more impressive.

MYSTIC FIVE

• • • • ☆ ☆ ☆ • • • •

All you require for this trick is a pack of ordinary playing cards.

Effect

A card is freely selected from the pack by a member of the audience. It is replaced in top position, and the pack is cut. The magician explains that one card will magically reverse itself in the pack, and its value will denote the position of the chosen card. When the pack is fanned, a card – for example, the five of hearts – is seen to be reversed, and believe it or not, the fifth card to follow it is the chosen one.

Apparatus

A pack of cards.

Set-up

Before the start of the presentation, remove a five-spot card, reverse it and replace it in the pack, so that it becomes the fifth card from the bottom of the pack.

Working and Presentation

Fan the pack making sure the audience is not aware of the reversed card. Request a spectator to select a card and then to return it to the top of the pack.

Make a complete cut of the pack bringing the reversed card towards the centre of the pack. Fan the pack to show the reversed card. State that the value of the reversed card will denote the exact position of the card selected by the spectator. Count along five cards and the fifth card will automatically be the chosen one.

Five-spot card

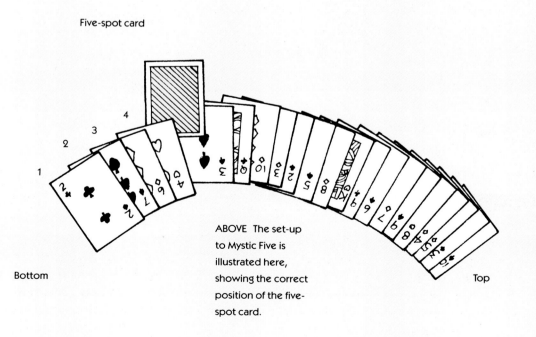

ABOVE The set-up to Mystic Five is illustrated here, showing the correct position of the five-spot card.

Bottom

Top

RED AND BLACK
SEPARATION

· · · · ☆ ☆ ☆ · · · ·

Here, the performer appears to accomplish the impossible, a
miracle which can be presented with a normal pack of cards, even
a borrowed one.

Effect

A pack of cards is shown to the audience
and shuffled. All 52 cards are spread face-
down on a table. Skilfully, the performer
divines the colour of each card, red or black.

Apparatus

A regular pack of cards.

Set-up

Before or during your magical performance,
secretly arrange the pack so that the red pip
cards are separated from the black ones.

With both blocks of cards separate, secretly
bend both, reds up and blacks down.

Working and Presentation

You will find that even when the cards are
shuffled together and then spread face-
down on the table, it is quite easy for you to
see which are the red cards and which are
the black. In divining the colour of each card,
simply point here and there, touching each
card and revealing their colours.

Afterwards, secretly remove the curves by
just flexing the pack.

ABOVE To set up
this trick, separate
the red pip cards
from the black ones,
and bend the red
block upwards and
the black
downwards, as
shown.

TRIPLE CARD DIVINATION
· · · · ☆ ☆ ☆ · · · ·

The performer will receive credit for being a clever diviner of cards
in this trick, one which can be performed in close-up and
surrounded by the audience.

Effect

A pack of cards is shuffled by a member of the audience and returned to the performer, who spreads them face-down on the table. Touching one face-down card, the performer states its suit and value – the card is placed to one side. Two other cards from the spread are pointed to by the performer, and their names are declared aloud. When all three cards are reversed they are found to be the ones that the magician divined.

Apparatus

A regular pack of cards.

Working and Presentation

Ask a member of the audience to shuffle the pack. Take the pack from the spectator and secretly glimpse at the bottom card of the pack and remember it. (For our purpose, the bottom card is the six of spades.) Spread the cards over the surface of the table, face-down. Although the cards may be spread haphazardly, you must be able to locate the card which was at the bottom of the pack.

In divining the first of the three cards, touch the back of any card stating it is a black card, a six – the six of spades – announcing the name of the bottom card. Remove the first card from the spread, but secretly note its value before placing it to the side. Touch a second card and announce the name of the first card just noted. Remove this second card, too, and place it to the side near the first one, again noting its value.

To divine the third card, touch the card which was originally at the bottom of the pack and announce the name of the second card just noted. Place this card with the other two.

Pick up and reverse all three cards to show that they are indeed the cards that you have just named.

LEFT How can you correctly divine the suit and value of three cards from a shuffled pack spread out, face-down, on a table? See above for the answer.

ELIMINATION

· · · · ☆ ☆ ☆ · · · ·

Magicians have been using elimination methods for many years. In the following trick, elimination is used to restrict a spectator's supposedly free choice.

Effect

The performer holds up a playing card to reveal only its back design. The card is placed inside an envelope, which is sealed and handed to a spectator.

A series of questions is directed towards the spectator, a quick answer each time coming back to the performer, until the name of a playing card is decided by the spectator himself. Needless to say, the card named by the spectator is the card that was placed inside the envelope.

Apparatus

An envelope and a playing card of any suit and value. The three of diamonds has been selected for the following example.

Working and Presentation

Display the back of the playing card to the audience and seal it inside the envelope. Then hand the envelope to a spectator to take charge of during the experiment. Obtain the services of a second spectator and begin a series of questions. 'Think of one of the colours – red or black?' The spectator answers red. If that is the colour of the card, and it is in our case, well and good, but if the spectator says black, reply, 'That leaves us with red'. Ask the second question. 'A picture or a plain card?' The spectator answers plain, and all is well. Once again, if the spectator answers picture, say, 'That leaves us with plain'.

Continue, 'Red was chosen, please mention one of the two suits, hearts or diamonds. If the spectator chooses diamonds say, 'Fine'; if he answers hearts, again use the elimination process saying 'That leaves us with diamonds'. Ask further 'Now, do you want high or low numbers?' If low numbers are requested, say 'Between ace and four, because the ace doesn't count, we are left with two or three.' If the spectator asks for three, you are fine, but if two is requested say 'That leaves us with three'. If the spectator asks for high numbers, the elimination works again, and you say that this leaves the low numbers. By this method you can always arrive at the card you first selected.

This trick can only be carried off with practice, and clear and quick thinking.

FAST FIND CARD TRICK

· · · · ☆ ☆ ☆ · · · ·

Finding a chosen card quickly, without fuss or bother, can often be a difficult task. The version which follows is not only cheeky in method but clever in performance.

Effect

A card is freely selected by a member of the audience, who then freely returns the card to any position in the pack. The performer immediately locates the spectator's chosen card.

Apparatus

A regular pack of cards and a pencil.

Set-up

Beforehand, and in secret, run a pencil line down one side of the pack; the line should be fairly light, but should be visible to you.

Working and Presentation

Fan the pack of cards, face-down, towards a spectator, and ask her to freely select a card. When the card has been removed and while it is being shown to members of the audience by the spectator, secretly turn the pack around before the selected card is returned. Because the pack has been reversed, the chosen card is the only card showing a pencil mark against the plain white edges of the rest of the pack. It is now an easy matter to break at that card and remove it to prove that it is indeed the chosen card.

LEFT In the set-up to
this trick, mark the
pack by running a
pencil line lightly
down one side of
the pack.

LEFT In
performance,
secretly turn the
pack round before
the spectator
replaces the card.
The chosen card is
immediately
apparent by its mark.

IN THE DARK

· · · · ☆ ☆ ☆ · · · ·

The audience will certainly be in the dark while watching this rather puzzling card miracle.

Effect

A pack of cards is well shuffled. A spectator is asked to freely select one card, but is told not to look at its identity at this stage of the procedure. To make it even more difficult, the room lights are switched off so that everything is in the dark. The chosen card is placed face down onto the palm of the spectator's hand. Dramatically, the performer announces the name of the chosen card. The experiment is repeated another two times with similar startling results.

Apparatus

A regular pack of cards.

Working and Presentation

This effect is best performed in a series of other card tricks. When the time comes, secretly palm off three cards from the pack, note their values and pocket them.

In performance ask the spectator to select a card but not to look at its suit or value at this stage. The lights are switched off and

LEFT The trick to this card effect is to secretly palm off three cards from the pack.

you take the card. In replacing the card onto the palm of the spectator's hand, secretly exchange the chosen card with one from the pocket. Of course, this is all done in the dark; unknown to the audience, a clever switch has been made.

Announce the value and suit of the chosen card. When the lights are switched on, and the spectator reverses the card, he finds it is the one which you have divined.

To avoid confusing the unwanted cards with the palmed cards within the pocket, a simple method of keeping them apart is to have a folded pocket handkerchief acting as a divider. Cards that are secretly placed into the pocket go on one side of the handkerchief and those that are being removed, on the other. This means that the card effect can be repeated several times without any complications arising.

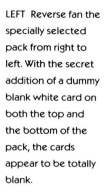

PRINTER'S DREAM

· · · · · ☆ ☆ ☆ · · · · ·

A printer's dream comes true in this effect.

Effect

The performer fans a pack of plain white cards showing the cards are really blank on both sides. When he next fans the cards towards the audience, the pack appears to be fully printed.

Apparatus

Believe it or not, a genuine pack of cards is required for this near miracle, although it is important that it should display indices on only two corners of each card and not four – some packs have the indices printed on all four corners. It is also important that the back design does not bleed off, but has a wide white border.

Also required are two double-blank playing cards (white on both sides). The performer can obtain these either from a complete pack from a magic dealer, or make them up by neatly covering the front and back of each of the jokers with white contact adhesive material.

Set-up

Have one double-blank card at the top of the pack and one at the bottom. Place the pack carefully into its case and you are all set to begin the performance.

Working and Presentation

Remove the cards from the case and 'reverse fan' the pack. In other words, instead of fanning the pack as normal, from left to right, fan from right to left. The reverse fan covers the indices, and with the blank white card on the face of the pack the whole pack appears to be blank. Because the pattern on the backs of the cards has a wide white border around each one, the other face of the fan appears blank, too.

LEFT Reverse fan the specially selected pack from right to left. With the secret addition of a dummy blank white card on both the top and the bottom of the pack, the cards appear to be totally blank.

LEFT Fan the same pack as normal, from left to right, to reveal normal printed cards. (Note the pack is printed with the indices in two corners only.)

Square up the pack, turn it face downwards, and remove the blank card from what is now the bottom of the pack. Show this card on both sides just as an additional flourish to convince the audience that each card is blank on both sides. Now replace this card, but on top of the other double-blank card, which is already in top position.

Now turn the pack over, wave your hand over the front card, and it appears to be printed. Fan the pack, but this time in the usual manner – from left to right – showing that the faces of the cards are now printed.

Cut the pack so that the two blank white cards are now approximately in the middle, then fan the cards to show the printed back designs. Be careful not to fully expose the two blank cards in the middle.

You have just printed a complete pack of blank cards by magic!

★ FORCING CARDS ★

There will be times when the performer may have to 'force' a card or cards onto a spectator to achieve some effects. While many methods rarely rely upon sleight of hand or dexterity, some do. For the benefit of the general magician wishing to learn these important techniques, the most practical have been included here.

★ FALSE SHUFFLING ★

From time to time you will rely upon what is known as false shuffling when performing some of the card effects described in this section. There are several methods of false shuffling — that is shuffling the pack in a convincing manner yet leaving all or most of the cards undisturbed. Here are two variations:

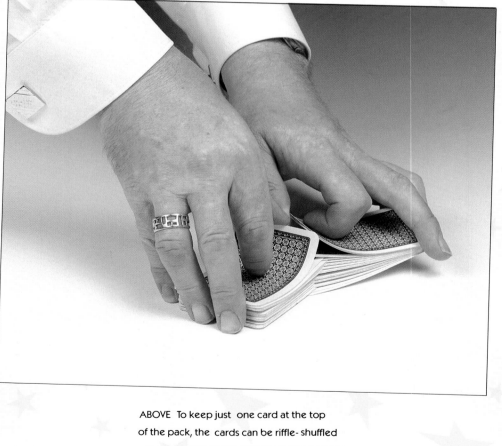

ABOVE To keep just one card at the top of the pack, the cards can be riffle-shuffled — the top card always remains in top position.

1 To keep several cards at the top of the pack in their original sequence, bring the top section from the rear to the front.

3 . . . return the cards at the back of this section to the top again. Repeat the procedure.

2 Drop some of the cards at the front of the top section into the other hand, but . . .

4 The topmost cards will always remain on top of the pack.

THE FAMOUS FAN FORCE

Effect

This force is probably the most convincing of all, simply because the pack is fanned and a spectator is asked to take a card. It eliminates unnecessary counts or covering the pack with a handkerchief, for example. Fairness and simplicity register firmly in the minds of the audience.

Apparatus

A pack of cards.

Set-up

The card required for forcing should be at the top of the pack. If false shuffled (see above), retain the card in top position.

Working and Presentation

Cut the pack so that the top card is now approximately in the centre, but under your control – use the little finger of the left hand to create a tiny break marking its position. This break position must be controlled throughout the movements which follow.

Approach the spectator, advancing slowly. Start fanning the cards, face-down, from the right to the left, peeling off cards as required. Watch for the spectator's reaction, his hand coming forwards to take a card. As his hand moves forwards to grasp one, either slow down or speed up the procedure so that the right card reaches his fingertips at the right time, without him realizing the selection is under your control. Such actions must be smooth and appear to look casual and fair, for as the cards flow from one hand to the other you are responsible for the judgement of your movements.

Should the spectator pass the planned card, quickly rush through the pack to the end, quipping that the spectator must be decisive, and start the procedure again.

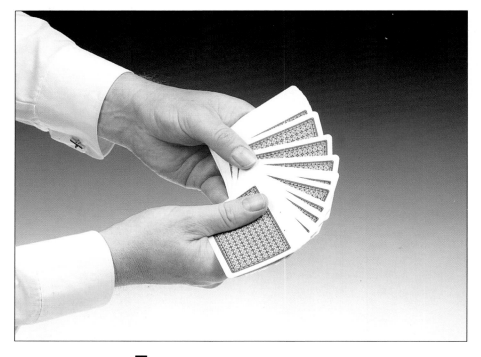

1 Slowly fan the cards from right to left as you approach the spectator.

2 Have the controlled card ready as the spectator is about to select.

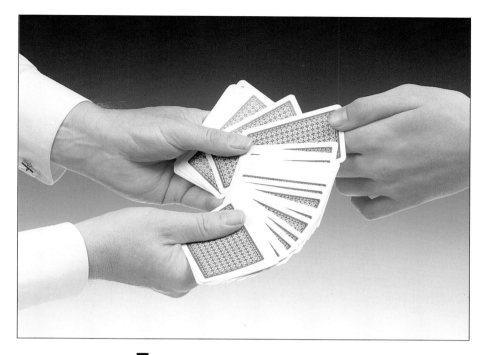

3 Force the controlled card into the spectator's hand as he or she reaches forwards.

IN THE PALM OF YOUR HAND
· · · · ☆ ☆ ☆ · · · ·

Students who would like to resort to sleight-of-hand methods to accomplish a card force may well appreciate this one. Study the sleight-of-hand techniques using card palms in Chapter 1 before attempting this trick.

Apparatus

A pack of cards.

Set-up

The card to be forced is on top of the pack.

Working and Presentation

False shuffle the pack, keeping the top card in top position. Grip the pack between the fingers and thumb of the right hand; in transferring it from the right hand to the left, allow the top card to pivot upwards into palm position. This is executed as the pack is placed on the table. Keep the palmed card in a natural hand position.

Ask a spectator to cut the pack into two piles. This being done, with the right hand (containing the concealed palmed card) casually reach over to lift up the bottom section of the cut. In doing so, add the palmed card to the top of this section of cards. Transfer these cards into the left hand once again. Ask the spectator to remove the card where the cut was made, and to reverse it, revealing its identity.

The beauty of this method is that a borrowed pack can be used, and that there is no previous preparation required.

★ EFFECTS USING THE ★ THUMB-TIP

PRODUCING A HANDKERCHIEF FROM THIN AIR
· · · · ☆ ☆ ☆ · · · ·

Effect

The magician shows both hands to be empty. Making a catching motion in the air, the performer forms his right hand into a clenched fist. From the fist is magically extracted a coloured silk handkerchief.

Apparatus

A thumb-tip and a small silk handkerchief.

Set-up

Secrete the handkerchief into the thumb-tip prior to the start of the effect, making sure one corner is towards the open end of the thumb-tip for easy extraction. The thumb-tip should be worn on the thumb.

Working and Presentation

To pleasing patter lines, show the hands to be empty in the manner previously described. Fingers and thumbs are wiggled, hands always on the move. With the right hand, reach into the air making a catching motion. In doing so, allow the thumb to bend inwards so that it is towards the palm of the hand, the fingers also coming inwards to form a fist. Withdraw the thumb. The thumb-tip is now firmly contained within the fist with its open mouth towards the top. With the first finger and thumb of the left hand, pull out the silk from the tip. From the

audience's viewpoint you appear to be extracting the silk from the fist itself.

There are two possible ways of discarding the thumb-tip after use. The first method is to allow the thumb to re-enter the tip so that it is back in its original position. The second method is executed when the silk is being displayed after its production. As the silk is discarded or pocketed, the thumb-tip secretly goes with it. This latter method is better than the first since your hands are genuinely empty, ready for the continuance of other effects which do not require the gadget.

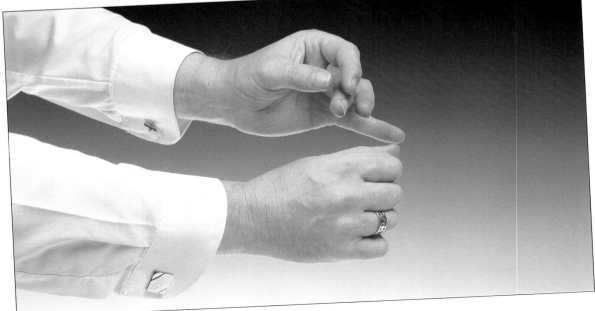

LEFT The thumb-tip has been secretly removed from the right thumb to be clutched, hidden, in the fist.

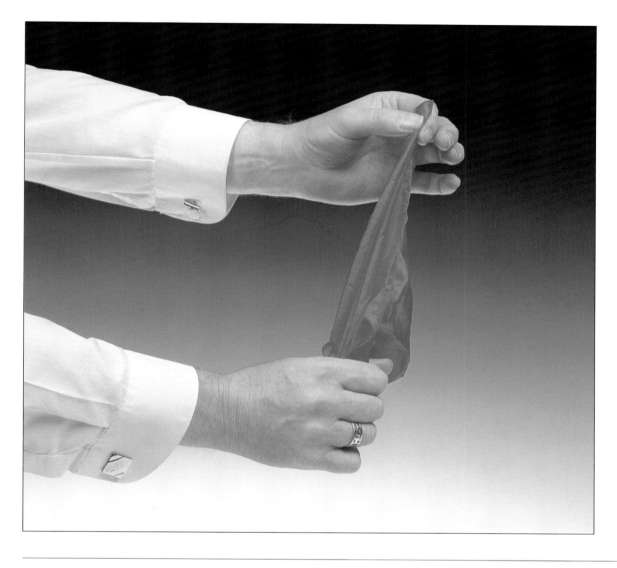

LEFT Now the silk handkerchief can be magically drawn from the fist.

VANISHING A SILK HANDKERCHIEF
· · · · ☆ ☆ ☆ · · · ·

Vanishing a handkerchief is as simple as producing it. The empty thumb-tip is already on the thumb at the start, or can be secretly obtained from the pocket.

Apparatus

A thumb-tip and a small silk handkerchief.

Working and Presentation

Show both hands to be empty and curl in the fingers and thumb of the right hand so as to make a fist. With the thumb-tip now removed from the thumb and held in the clenched fist, tuck the silk into the hidden thumb-tip.

Once the silk is inside, it is an easy matter to insert the thumb back into the tip so that both hands can then be opened to show that the silk has completely vanished.

STIFF'N ROPE
· · · · · ☆ ☆ ☆ · · · · ·

A touch of magic from India, this platform item resembles the theme of the Indian Rope Trick.

Effect

A length of rope is balanced on the end of the first finger, and magically becomes rigid. It then assumes its original limp form after the trick has been accomplished.

Apparatus

A length of soft white rope.

Set-up

Sew a small loop of flesh-coloured cotton thread to one end of the rope.

Working and Presentation

With the right hand, hold the end of the rope, concealing the loop of thread. To balance the end of the rope on the left first finger, slip this finger into the loop and with the right hand, hold the opposite end of the rope upwards. The rope becomes stiff and rigid. Pull the hands against each other to ensure that the rope is kept taut.

To complete the trick, disengage the finger from the loop and the length of rope resumes its original form.

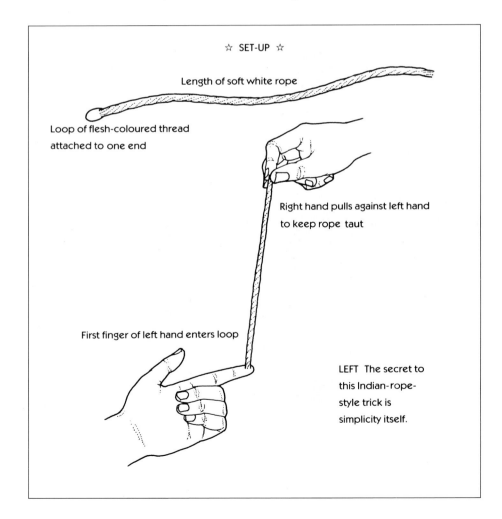

☆ SET-UP ☆

Length of soft white rope

Loop of flesh-coloured thread attached to one end

Right hand pulls against left hand to keep rope taut

First finger of left hand enters loop

LEFT The secret to this Indian-rope-style trick is simplicity itself.

CURRENCY-CUT
· · · · · ☆ ☆ ☆ · · · · ·

Effect

A borrowed bank note is slid inside a flat tube of paper. The audience clearly sees the paper currency through the two windows cut out at each end. The tube and bank note are cut in half with a pair of scissors, yet moments later the note is pulled from the wreckage, undamaged and apparently restored.

Apparatus

A paper tube made from a long narrow envelope. Seal the envelope, then cut a strip off each end to form a tube. Now cut two slits in the rear of the tube about 5 cm (2 in) apart, they must be long enough to allow the bank note to slide through them. Cut out two square window shapes from the front of the flat tube.

Set-up

Have the paper tube nearby, with the slit side facing downwards, together with a pair of scissors.

Working and Presentation

Borrow a bank note and slide it through the paper tube so that it comes out the opposite end. Push it back inside again, this time forcing it out through one slit and back into the tube through the other slit, so that the central portion of the bank note is outside the paper tube. The audience can clearly see the note through the cut-out windows in the front face of the tube.

Cut through the centre of the tube, but slide the scissors behind the note, so that you only cut the tube. Hold together both cut sections as you quickly pull out the five pound note and show it to be restored. Crumple or cut up the paper tube to destroy the evidence.

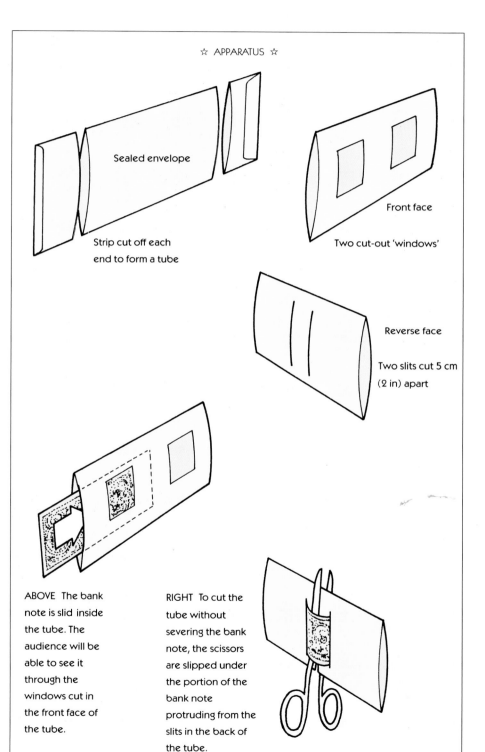

☆ APPARATUS ☆

Sealed envelope

Strip cut off each end to form a tube

Front face

Two cut-out 'windows'

Reverse face

Two slits cut 5 cm (2 in) apart

ABOVE The bank note is slid inside the tube. The audience will be able to see it through the windows cut in the front face of the tube.

RIGHT To cut the tube without severing the bank note, the scissors are slipped under the portion of the bank note protruding from the slits in the back of the tube.

THE MULTIPLYING BILLIARD BALLS

· · · · ☆ ☆ ☆ · · · · ·

Often sold in more advanced boxes of magic, this is usually one of the first tricks the beginner learns.

Effect

The performer reaches into the air; a red billiard ball materializes. It multiplies to two, to three and then to four, all four balls being displayed between the fingers. The balls can be made to vanish singly, transpose and reappear elsewhere, at will.

Apparatus

The set comprises three solid balls and one shell (a hollow half-ball). The shell is especially made to fit over any of the three balls. It is a good idea to paint the balls with red lacquer, as this colour allows audiences large and small to see the balls clearly during the performance. A silk handkerchief is also required.

Set-up

Place one ball, with the shell over it, in the right trouser pocket. Place the second ball inside the left trouser pocket. Place the third ball in the left jacket pocket with the silk handkerchief.

Working and Presentation

The pivoting move, on which this sequence relies, may at first seem awkward to the beginner, but constant practice, preferably in front of a mirror, will enable anyone to master these moves and present a polished performance.

☆ **PRODUCING TWO BILLIARD BALLS** ☆

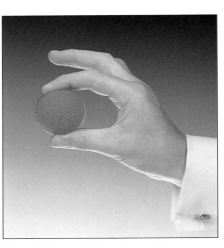

1 With the right hand casually resting in the right trouser pocket, palm the ball with the shell over it. Remove the hand from the pocket and pluck this ball out of the air to appear between the thumb and the first finger. Show it on both sides as one ball.

2 Lower the second finger of the right hand to pivot the solid ball out from the shell . . .

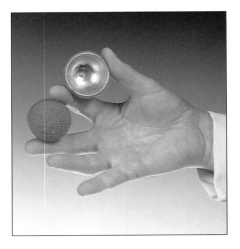

3 . . . like this.

4 To the audience you appear to be holding two solid balls.

☆ THE VANISH ☆

Raise the left hand as if to take away the ball gripped between the first and second fingers, but in fact use it as a shield to conceal the following move. Under cover make a clutching motion with the right hand, allowing the ball to pivot back inside the shell.

Withdraw the closed left fist, supposedly holding a ball, from the right hand, where one solid ball appears to remain, gripped between the thumb and first finger. Slowly open the left hand to reveal that it is empty.

☆ PRODUCING THREE BILLIARD BALLS ☆

Reach inside the left trouser pocket with the left hand, removing the planted ball. As you position this ball between the first and second fingers of the right hand, quickly pivot out the ball within the shell to be held between the second and third fingers. Three balls have now been magically produced.

☆ ANOTHER VANISH ☆

Shield the centre ball with the left hand, pretending to remove it from its position. As you appear to grasp it, pivot the ball back inside the shell.

This time pretend to place the ball, supposedly in the left hand, into your mouth. As your clenched fist moves up in front of your mouth, press the tongue against the side of the cheek so that it looks as if the mouth is holding the ball.

Show that the left hand is empty, and with the first finger push the 'bulge' inwards, as if swallowing the ball.

☆ PRODUCING FOUR BILLIARD BALLS ☆

Reach inside the left jacket pocket with the left hand and produce the ball planted there. Place it firmly between the third and fourth fingers of the right hand and show the three balls on both sides.

Produce the final fourth ball from within the shell, as before, using the pivoting action, so that it now takes its place between the first and second fingers.

☆ MORE VANISHES ☆

Vanish two balls as follows. Show the right hand holding the four balls. Shake your hand in the air and one ball appears to have vanished – you have pivoted the ball between the first and second fingers inside the shell, leaving three in view. Show both sides of the remaining balls to the audience.

With the left hand move the ball between the second and third fingers and reposition it between the first and second fingers of the right hand. Under cover of this move 'steal' away the ball from within the shell with the left hand – simply allow the ball to drop out of the shell and into the awaiting clenched fist. Make a second vanish with the right hand – pivoting the ball now held between the first and second fingers into the shell – and at the same time secretly pocket the unwanted ball from the left hand.

Now remove the ball from between the third and fourth fingers and place it between the first and second fingers. In doing this, again 'steal' away the ball from within the shell with the left hand as before.

☆ A QUICK TRANSPOSITION ☆

Drop the left hand, formed in a fist, beside the body, with the back of the hand towards the audience. Similarly, lower the right hand, containing what appear to be two solid balls, of which one is really the shell.

With a throwing motion of the right hand, vanish the solid ball held between the first and second fingers, secretly pivoting it inside the shell. Simultaneously, produce the palmed ball within the left hand – a rather neat transposition.

☆ HANDKERCHIEF VANISH ☆

Place this ball between the first and second fingers of the right hand and, under cover, steal away the one inside the shell.

Reach inside the left jacket pocket and remove the silk handkerchief; at the same time deposit the ball taken from the shell into the pocket. With the left hand hold the silk by one corner, draping it over both balls, and then reach beneath, supposedly to take one away. In fact, pivot the ball into the shell, and withdraw the left hand as if holding the ball.

Slowly open the fingers of the left hand to show the ball has vanished and then remove the handkerchief to show that only one ball remains in the right hand. Pocket the handkerchief; the remaining ball, together with the shell, can be vanished by any of the sleight-of-hand methods.

The routine should end, as it began, with the hands completely empty.

UNEQUAL ROPES

· · · · ☆ ☆ ☆ · · · ·

Of all the rope tricks popular with audiences, Unequal Ropes is
probably one of the best.

Effect

The performer displays three different lengths
of rope: one very short, one medium length
and a long piece; side by side their differences are apparent.

The ends of the ropes are brought up to
meet the opposite ends, and while the
magician states that the three lengths are
now the same, the audience clearly sees that
the centres are not. The magician takes the
ends of the ropes in each hand and magically 'stretches' them, so that all three become
the same length. Furthermore, the lengths are
counted singly, proving the point.

The ends of the ropes are once again
placed end to end, blown onto, and mysteriously return to their original lengths, one
short, one medium and one long.

Apparatus

Three different lengths of rope. The ropes
must be identical in appearance and colour,
but there should be a short piece, a medium
piece twice as long as the short piece and a
long piece three times as long as the short
piece. Keep the three lengths knotted together ready for the presentation – you will
avoid losing one of them at the vital moment.

Working and Presentation

1 Unknot the ropes and display them to
the audience in order of length to
emphasize their differences: first, hold up
the short length and then place it in the
left hand; then the medium length,
placing it in the left hand to the right of
the short length; and finally the long
length, placing it in the left hand to the
right of the medium length.

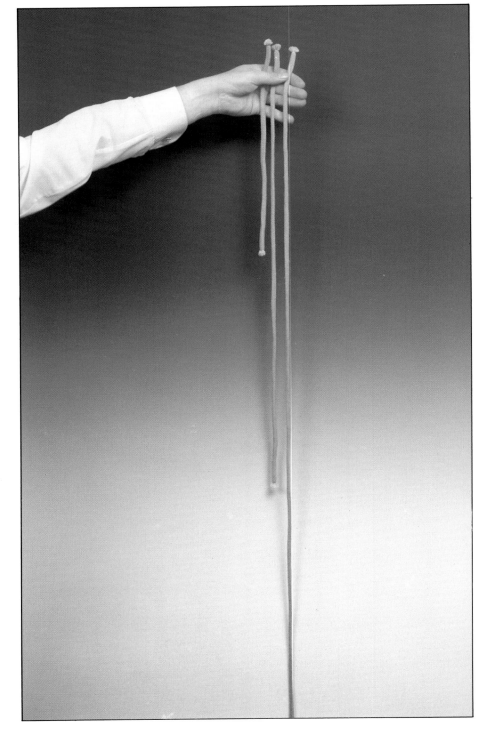

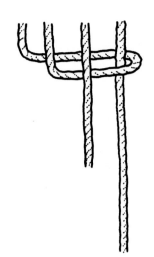

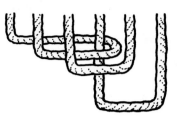

4 Bring the free end of the long length up and place it in the left hand to the right of the other lengths. Six ends are now held in the left hand.

2 Pass the right hand between the medium and the long lengths, take hold of the short length and bring it through, over the long length and then round the back of all the lengths so that the free end is brought into the left hand and held to the left of the other ends. Four ends are now held in the left hand.

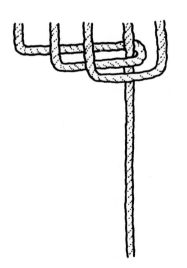

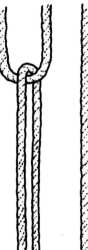

6 Drop the ends from the right hand and hold the ropes up in the left hand – the fingers of the left hand curling round and concealing the looped joins in the ropes.

5 You are now ready to 'stretch' the ropes into equal lengths. With the right hand, take the three ends lying on the right; retain the three ends lying on the left in the left hand. Pull the ropes taut, all three pieces of rope actually appear to be the same length.

3 Bring the free end of the medium length up and place it in the left hand to the right of the other lengths. Five ends are now held in the left hand.

✩ COUNTING THE ROPES ✩

The lengths of rope can now be counted and shown separately. With the right hand, remove the one separate length (the original medium length) and display it, counting 'one'. Go to pick up a second length, secretly depositing the separate length and removing the two linked lengths, counting 'two'. Finally, pick up the separate length again and count 'three'. The audience believes they have seen three separate ropes, each of equal length.

✩ REVERSING THE EFFECT ✩

1 Bring the free end of the separate length and place it in the left hand to the left of the other ends.

2 Bring the left-hand portion of the long linked length up to the left.

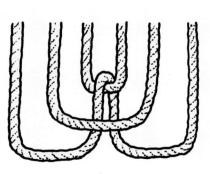

3 Bring the right hand portion up to the right.

4 Take the first three ends on the right in the right hand, and simultaneously drop the remaining ends from the left hand and give the ropes a dramatic shake. They automatically separate to return to their original lengths: one short, one medium and one long.

BAFFLING BALLOONS
· · · · ☆ ☆ ☆ · · · ·

This is an unusual effect using items that are easily obtainable.

Effect

Two paper bags are shown, one with a red spot on the front, the other sporting a green spot. They are examined by members of the audience. Two balloons are then produced, one red and one green, and dropped inside the corresponding bag. A snap of the fingers, and the red balloon is pulled from the green-spot bag and the green balloon from the red-spot bag – a neat transposition.

Apparatus

Four balloons, two of each colour, red and green; two paper bags; two coloured spots, one green and one red.

Set-up

Stick the coloured spots on the front of each of the paper bags. Push a green balloon inside a red one, using the blunt end of a pencil. Allow part of the neck of the inner balloon to protrude. The second red balloon is pushed inside the other green one in a similar fashion.

Working and Presentation

Let the audience examine the empty paper bags. Display the balloons and place them inside the bags, so that the colours of the balloons match the coloured spots. Hide the necks of the inner balloons with your fingers. Then wave a magic wand, or snap the fingers to make the effect more magical. Remove the first bag from the table, holding it firmly by the base with the fingers gripping the balloon inside through the paper. With the right hand reach inside the bag and pull out the inner balloon of a different colour. Crush the bag, containing the original outer balloon, and cast aside. Repeat with the second bag and balloon to show that both have magically transposed.

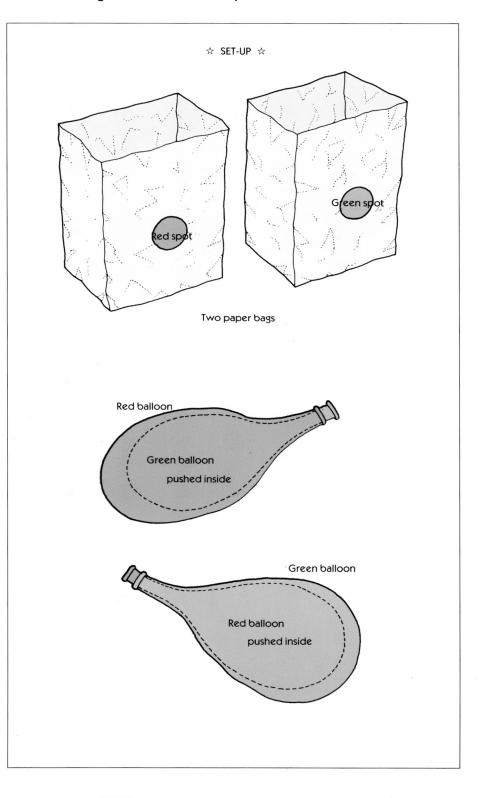

THE FAMOUS CUT AND RESTORED ROPE

· · · · ☆ ☆ ☆ · · · ·

Magicians have been cutting and restoring ropes for more years than I can possibly remember, as this is regarded as one of the greatest of all the classics of magic. This version is perhaps one of the simplest, and the preset arrangement provided makes for easier handling.

Effect

A length of soft white rope is doubled up, severed in the centre, shown as two pieces, and then magically restored to its original whole state.

Apparatus

A length of soft white rope; it is best to use magicians' rope, which is manufactured without the usual central core. A small loop of similar rope is also required. The ends of this short length can either be sewn together or bound with adhesive tape. A pair of sharp scissors. It is important to wear a watch and a jacket in this version.

Set-up

Push the ends of the loop of rope under the watch-strap so that the loop lies against the inner wrist. The cuff of the jacket covers this arrangement. Have the scissors and the length of rope on the table in front of you.

Working and Presentation

Display the length of rope by tugging it between the hands to prove it is one strong piece. Furthermore, allow a spectator to examine it. Hold the rope suspended in the left hand. With the right hand, locate the middle of the rope, and double the length up. As the looped portion of the doubled rope is brought up into the left hand, pull away the secreted loop of rope from the watch-strap and bring it up into the left hand. To the audience it appears that the centre of the length of rope is protruding

from your clenched left hand. Pick up the scissors with the right hand, and, with one definite cut, sever the dummy loop centrally. Then state that you will trim the ends of the rope, and proceed to do this, allowing the bits to fall to the floor. With the centre of the genuine rope still clenched within the left hand, simply blow on the rope and show that it is miraculously restored.

1 With the dummy loop secretly tucked into the watch-strap against the inner wrist, display the length of rope to the audience.

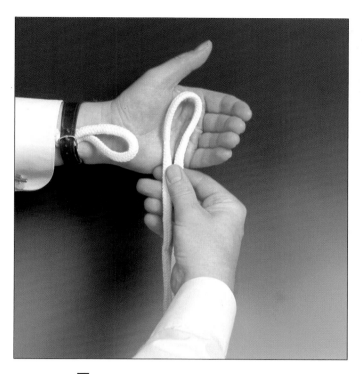

2 Locate the centre of the rope with the right hand, double it up and bring the looped portion into the left hand.

4 . . . bring it up through the fingers of the left hand.

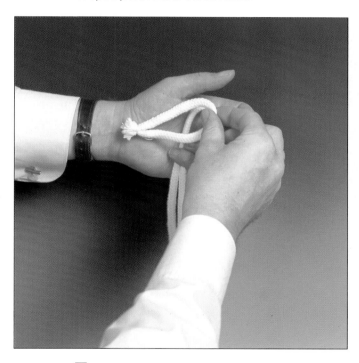

3 Secretly withdraw the dummy loop from the watch-strap and . . .

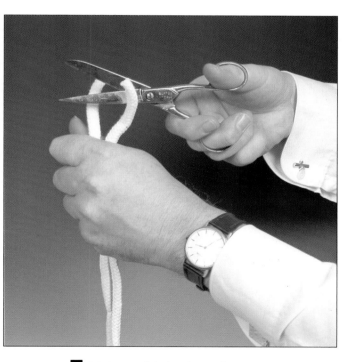

5 It is impossible for the audience to detect that this loop is not part of the original length of rope. Cut the dummy loop.

THE CLASSIC EGG BAG

• • • • ☆ ☆ ☆ • • • •

The famous Egg Bag trick was a feature of Arnold de Biere's music hall act; it was also a hit in the show *How's Tricks* presented by Australian-born Les Levante.
The trick lends itself to comedy presentation and can be performed at close quarters without detection. Furthermore, during the routine a number of magical things happen and there is plenty of audience participation involved.

Effect

A flat cloth bag is shown to the audience from all sides, inside and out – the bag appears to be empty, yet moments later an egg appears inside. The egg is made to vanish, reappear and finally find its way into a spectator's pocket.

Apparatus

A specially made cloth bag. The bag is faked so that while it has an inside and an outside, there is a secret pocket on one of the inside faces. This pocket has an opening towards the bottom. It is there both to conceal the egg and then later to allow the egg to drop into the bag proper.

You also require an imitation egg which can be made of plastic or wood. Some rubber joke eggs, available from joke and novelty stores, are ideal for this purpose. Experience has shown that a blown egg is not suitable for this presentation.

Set-up

Conceal the faked egg inside the secret pocket in the bag.

Working and Presentation

Lift the bag from the table, show both sides, then turn it inside out. To do this, grip the egg through the material of the bag as you turn the bag inside out. The egg will stay inside the bag during this procedure and all looks quite convincing – you appear to be holding an ordinary cloth bag. However, when showing the inside of the bag, always keep the side with the pocket towards the body and away from the audience. Turn the bag right side out again and you are ready to start the routine.

LEFT The classic egg bag seen right side out.

LEFT Now inside out, the secret pocket can be seen. Always keep this face of the bag towards you when displaying the classic egg bag.

Announce that you will produce an egg from the empty bag, using the magic word 'Eggstraordinary'. Say the magic word and place the empty right hand inside the bag. At the time time, release the left hand's grip of the egg through the material of the bag allowing the egg to drop out of its secret pocket into the bag. With a flourish, withdraw the right hand to reveal the egg.

Replace the egg inside the bag and ask a selected spectator to shout out the magic word 'Eggstraordinary'. This being done, invert the bag. Of course, nothing falls out because, in turning the bag mouth downwards towards the floor, the egg automatically drops into the pocket. The egg appears to have vanished. However, to make it even more convincing, turn the bag inside out as before, showing the inside to be empty and then bring the bag back to its original position. Now place the empty right hand inside the bag and reproduce the egg, showing it to the audience.

Next, put the egg back inside the bag, utter the magic word, and swish the right hand around inside the bag. Pretend to remove the egg, gripping the fist closed, and further pretend to secrete it under the left armpit. Continue with the presentation. Turn the bag inside out and back again showing that the egg has completely vanished, and when cries of 'it's under your arm' are heard, ignore them at first. Eventually, lift the right arm, showing that the egg is not there. The audience is not impressed. Lift the left arm showing that the egg is not there either. Then hold the bag open in both hands, and ask the spectator to reach inside and bring out the egg, which he does.

This could well be the climax of the effect but the more adventurous magician may wish to add something extra to give the routine a sting in the tail. Ask the spectator to open up the side pocket of the jacket he is wearing; tip the egg inside, or so it appears to the audience. In fact, when the bag is

tilted, the egg rolls into the secret pocket and stays there. Tip the bag, mouth towards the floor, to prove that it is empty.

Turn the bag inside out with mouth upwards, so that the egg falls out of the pocket and into the right hand. Palm the egg in this hand and casually take it away while misdirecting attention towards the spectator's pocket. Ask if he still has the egg; the spectator reaches inside his pocket to find that the egg has mysteriously vanished. Look inside the spectator's pocket too and agree, but as this is being done, secretly drop the palmed egg into the pocket.

Pretend to try and make the egg reappear back inside the bag but without success. Try again and reach inside to bring out what you call an invisible egg, holding it between the fingers and thumb of the right hand.

Make a movement as if to toss the egg into the spectator's pocket. Ask the spectator to remove the egg from his pocket himself and drop it inside the bag, completing the routine.

20TH-CENTURY SILKS

• • • • ☆ ☆ ☆ • • • •

Ask any practising magician to explain the working details of this trick and he will immediately know, for 20th-Century Silks has become a classic magical effect.

Effect

Two purple silk handkerchiefs are displayed and knotted together. A third silk of contrasting colour is shown and vanished, only to reappear tied and knotted between the other two.

Apparatus

A special set of silk handkerchiefs. This consists of a bag made from a purple silk square folded diagonally and sewn around the open edges, leaving a small opening at the top corner, as illustrated.

A purple silk handkerchief to match the above; a yellow silk handkerchief; and a yellow handkerchief to match the above but with a purple corner.

Set-up

Take the particoloured silk square and knot the yellow corner, diagonally opposite the purple one, to the open corner of the silk bag. Tuck the yellow handkerchief (with the purple corner) inside the purple silk bag, allowing the purple corner to protrude. The handkerchief is hidden inside during the presentation. Gather together the other two handkerchiefs so it appears that only three are being used.

Working and Presentation

First, pick up the two purple silks (one of which is the bag) and knot one corner of the purple silk to the false purple corner protruding from the silk bag. Tuck both silk handkerchiefs into a clear tumbler, with their corners hanging over the edge. Display the yellow silk handkerchief and make it vanish. Some performers use cones, boxes, tubes, etc to facilitate such a vanish, but the trouser

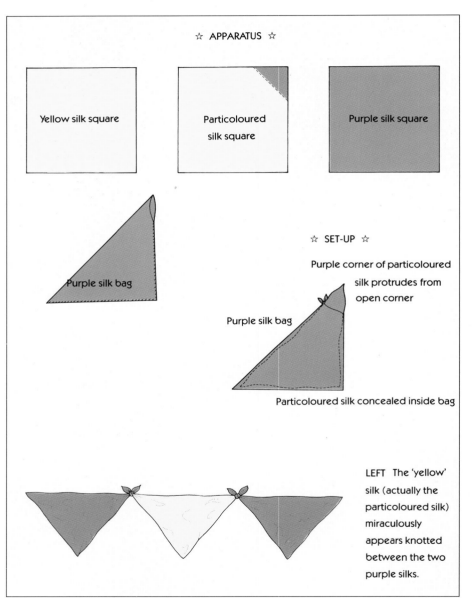

☆ APPARATUS ☆

Yellow silk square

Particoloured silk square

Purple silk square

Purple silk bag

☆ SET-UP ☆

Purple corner of particoloured silk protrudes from open corner

Purple silk bag

Particoloured silk concealed inside bag

LEFT The 'yellow' silk (actually the particoloured silk) miraculously appears knotted between the two purple silks.

pocket is just as effective. Place the silk handkerchief inside the pocket, and after uttering some magic words, pull out the lining of the pocket to show the vanish. The handkerchief has, in fact, been pushed up into the top section of the pocket. When the lining is turned out, the handkerchief is secured there and out of view.

Coming back to the silk handkerchiefs inside the tumbler, take the unattached corner of the standard purple silk and pull it away to show that the missing yellow silk has miraculously reappeared now firmly tied between the other two.